A GRAIN OF RICE

A GRAIN OF RICE

POETRY BY

EVELYN LAU

OOLICHAN BOOKS
FERNIE, BRITISH COLUMBIA, CANADA
2012

Library and Archives Canada Cataloguing in Publication

Lau, Evelyn, 1971-

A grain of rice / Evelyn Lau.

Poems.

ISBN 978-0-88982-286-3

I. Title.

PS8573.A7815G73 2012   C811'.54   C2012-905743-6

We gratefully acknowledge the financial support of the Canada Council for the Arts, the British Columbia Arts Council through the BC Ministry of Tourism, Culture, and the Arts, and the Government of Canada through the Canada Book Fund, for our publishing activities.

Published by
Oolichan Books
P.O. Box 2278
Fernie, British Columbia
Canada V0B 1M0

www.oolichan.com

for John Updike,
with gratitude for his work

Contents

Part One: Fortune

Fortune / 11
Snow Globe City / 12
The Night Market / 13
The #4 Bus / 14
City Centre / 15
Noise / 17
Downtown Life During the 2010 Olympics (or, Sleepless in Yaletown) / 19
After the Gold Medal Hockey Win, 2010 Olympics / 21
Ishq'allah / 23
Blue Heron / 25
What Was Lost (or, Bungling the Interview for the Position of Poet Laureate) / 27
Willow / 28
A Grain of Rice / 30
Frozen / 32
Reading Fiona Lam's Enter the Chrysanthemum / 33
Grandmother / 36

Part Two: Dear Updike

On Looking Into John Updike's Endpoint / 41
Updike Redux / 43
Dear Updike / 45
Updike in Pennsylvania / 46
Hospice of the North Shore, Danvers, MA / 48
Thinking of U(pdike) / 50

Part Three: Lost and Found

Swimming Lessons / 53
Honolulu / 54
Maui / 56
Sedona Blues / 58
Las Vegas / 60
Christmas Day, Cannon Beach / 61
Best Western / 62
Lost and Found / 64
Guanacaste Journal / 66

Part Four: Fear of Falling

English Bay / 73
Summerland / 74
The Music of Wreckage / 76
Life After Death / 78
The Beginning of Spring / 79
Memorial / 80
Vertigo / 81
Blue Lagoon / 82
Fear of Falling / 83
Waiting / 85
To a Friend Near the End / 87
Midlife / 89

Acknowledgements

Part One:
Fortune

Happiness. Is it a subject? It is best seen out of the corner of the eye.
— John Updike, "On Being a Self Forever"

FORTUNE

Today on the seawall, the wind spraying
my clothes with stars of salt, the ocean

boiling to a cream froth around blue rocks,
I remember that a man drowned in English Bay,

swimming off one of the rusty freighters,
striking out for this golden shore —

what a paradise this must have seemed to him,
our soft sloping mountains and clean wide sidewalks,

a dream of heaven he reached for and reached for
until the freezing waters swept his body ashore.

SNOW GLOBE CITY

Weeks of snow. The plants freeze, green leaves
darken to raisin, curl at the edges as if scorched.
The ink in my pen thickens, won't write.
At night we lie under a snowdrift
of duvets, not moving, conserving
the flickering flame of heat in our bodies —
one wrong move and it's bare skin
on a patch of ice. The fire in my brain all night,
the conflagration. Five blocks away
a homeless woman burns in her cart,
the stingy heat of a candle lighting up
her quilts and cardboard, her long red hair.
The most beautiful thing I've seen —
a rose of flame blossoming in blue water,
in snow. The crack and splinter of ice,
a canopy of powder slipping to the sidewalk —
you love how it muffles everything,
stifles the sounds of the city, the gunshots
going off downtown, the screams.

The metal grid burning. Fluff in the air.
The eiderdown sky. Bundled strangers passing,
eyes down, Styrofoam cups steaming
in their hands. Pyramids of coats and hats
and gloves and scarves; goose feathers in my nose.
Tomorrow the bridge will be coated in ice
the colour of concrete —
we will slip and slide across, cautious
as the elderly, oyster-grey ocean sluggish below.
A swipe of charcoal on a cement wall
the only record of the woman's passing,
the ghost shape of her life as it went up in flames.

THE NIGHT MARKET

In the night market, a woman with filthy hair
and clothes dripping with threads
stares at the vats of curried fish balls
and braised tripe as if at a storefront window
in Beverly Hills, her face squeezed by hunger.
Around her, hordes of families and couples,
lips shining with grease, reach for the next reward —
even the teenage girls on diets
pinch skewers of quail or scallop
between manicured nails.
I wish I could feed this stranger
like the baby seagull we found one day
in the bushes by the water, so docile or damaged
it let us put our hands on its body, suffering our touch
with eyes blank as beads
in exchange for a morsel. I could buy her
a meal and not miss it. Instead
we gorge on dumplings and waffles,
the starch sloshing in my stomach
like wet cement as the crowd roars past,
goldfish mouths flapping, the sky raining down
bitter black ash, soot in my nose and throat
from the cooking fires. This is the Richmond
Night Market on a Saturday, our stomachs straining
at our waistbands, bodies bathed in smoke
and spices, the sunset a tanker explosion
spilling across an oil-soaked sea. I stuff shrimp gyoza,
squid tentacles, kimchi pancakes
into my mouth as if into someone starving,
someone I am trying to save.

THE #4 BUS

I thought I saw him on the bus today.
It was in Kitsilano, on the #4,
the glass-fronted stores streaming past,
the yummy mummies wearing Lululemon
parading down the sidewalk, juggling lattes and SUV strollers
in the scrubbed sunshine. His clawed hands
which had dug into me, scraped between my legs
like steel instruments, were twisted arthritic
in his lap. I recognized the beaked nose,
the cheeks now sunken and stained
like watermarked parchment, the straggle of hair.

I looked away furiously, afraid
he would feel my glance like a hand
stroked against his skin, that I would have
gone and started it again. Headed blind
for the back doors, fire ants swarming my face.
Not that he'd recognize me now, at 37
plump and pedestrian, features beginning
their slow muddy sag into middle age —
no longer the drug-starved teen in tie-dye,
eyes kaleidoscoped from the painkillers I swallowed
to stand the thrust of his greedy hands.

How I had smiled in sympathy and said nothing
when he told the story of his toddler daughter
taking his penis into her mouth —
She was at that age, she'd grab anything
and put it in her mouth, I didn't want to give her a complex
by saying no. Nearly a quarter of a century later
I stood on the sidewalk outside Capers,
the bus pulling away, the flame-red trees spouting
gouts of blood into the salt air off Jericho.

14

CITY CENTRE

In this neighbourhood I've lived
through fifteen years of construction and destruction
on a downtown street choked with the debris of progress,
clouds of dust barrelling down the road

like Mack trucks, clogging my throat like fur.
I squint my eyes against the peppery sting of it,
the painful watering, pray my way
across the blind intersection, the souls of expired buildings

like soft grey shrouds smothering the air.
How soon we forget what used to be there —
the eccentric's clapboard house with its yard
of painted birdhouses, now a glossy condo;

after forty years of rising property taxes
he finally moved, died a month later. His neighbour
across the street stuck it out a decade longer
in a cottage next door to a nightclub,

weak roses straggling the barbed wire fence,
her taxes so steep she cancelled cable
and newspaper, couldn't afford the luxury
of a new lipstick or quilt for winter —

dwarfed by the forest of highrises, she would patrol
the street in front of her house, head wrapped
in a kerchief, black dog slinking at her feet.
Months after she moved, someone left a card

sealed in plastic, decorated with limp streamers,
tacked to the developer's fence around her house
with its drooping sashes and shattered attic window:
Happy birthday, little green house.

NOISE

Rage seeps into the hallways,
scraps of old battles re-heated —
fragments of fury, shouts through slammed doors,
footfalls pounding down like blows.
We apartment-dwellers think we live
in concrete cells, but our lives leak into our neighbours' —
the stifling stench of our cooking, meaty stews
and fried onions and the sour stink
of sauerkraut spooned from the jar,
the deliveryman's pepperoni pizza
trailing out the elevator into the fusty corridor.
My upstairs neighbour's 4 am rants:
F you, f you, f you,
chanted like a holy mantra,
creaky window cranked shut like a car backfiring,
mysterious thumps and thuds and the heart-stopping
smash of glass on tile. His bathroom visits in deep night
the downpour of a waterfall into a still pond —
I dream of burst pipes, floodwater, and wake
to him squeezing out the last yellow drops.
The inevitable music and sex —
a bass thumping in the distance like the first warning
of a headache, a headboard knocking
on a bedroom wall, a woman's wail in the night air:
I love you, I love you, I love you.
A hundred neighbours renovating,
one suite at a time —
jackhammers chipping out tile,
the hammering down of hardwood.
Earplugs become the only portal to sleep —
at last I could lie in bed

and listen to the sounds of my own body,
the rivulets of blood trickling through my veins,
the faint clicking in my jaw,
the soft animal snoring of my heart.

DOWNTOWN LIFE DURING THE 2010 OLYMPICS (or, Sleepless in Yaletown)

Air horns, cowbells. The national anthem
hoarsely roared by drunk revellers at three AM;
two hours later, dump trucks clanging and banging
through the alleys like furious beasts.
Fireworks like dropped bombs —
my elderly friend Ron
says the searchlights slicing up the sky at English Bay,
the hovering helicopters, remind him of the war.
Stoned with sleeplessness. The weather a wonderland
of trance-blue skies, stained glass tulips,
pink smog of cherry blossoms.
Waves of junk food odours sail on the breeze,
grease and vinegar from platters of poutine,
flaps of pizza drooling with microwave cheese,
beards of bristly candy floss.
Outside BC Place, I am swept into a sea
of red, a mass of strangers
wearing flags like superhero capes,
faces aglitter with maple leaves,
all bared teeth and whirligig eyes.
Drums beating, chests heaving.
Scarf of pot smoke hanging in the air.
We run a gauntlet of hawkers, their hands
like the disembodied hands reaching
from the walls of a haunted house,
thrusting out tickets for sale! Signs and souvenirs!
Athletes on billboards, bus shelters, high-def TV —
their babyish, half-formed faces
draped in medals and patriotism,
dazzled and half-blind in the spotlight,

in their fleet and vanishing prime.
Their frozen moment.
All night, the pulse from the hordes on Granville Street.
The chant, the clamour, the hoot and holler.
Pray for the annihilating silence of rain.

AFTER THE GOLD MEDAL HOCKEY WIN, 2010 OLYMPICS

I am in bed reading the saddest stories,
a collection by Chinese women writers
of the 1920's and 30's. And that's just the stories.
Then there are the authors' biographies,
matter-of-fact sketches of lives interrupted —
Ding Ling's eight years in prison,
twelve years of hard labour in the countryside;
Feng Keng's execution by the Kuomintang
at the age of 24; Lu Yin and Luo Shu's deaths in childbirth.
Outside, the city explodes, and keeps exploding.
World peace would not cause such jubilation.
Even the birds scatter in fright at this storm of noise —
seagulls sob, crows shake in their trees,
flap in a cloud of cacophony.
Geese veer into the panicked sky.
The streets are bleeding
with red, horns blaring, screams
not even the dying could summon.
Figures stream out of buildings
carrying pots and pans
like refugees fleeing on foot.

I walk to Sunset Beach, batter my body
against the flag-draped masses, lost
inside the roar that reverberates from all directions.
Such noise, the heart thinks it's an emergency.
Celebrants on balconies and bridges,
faces drenched in paint and sweat;
strangers' hands tearing at my sleeve,
pleading in vain for a hug, a high-five.

I reach the shoreline at last, the mosaic of shattered shells.
Watch a tourist cup his palm and dip it
into the Pacific, raise the brine to his lips and drink.
The glass-clear water washes
and washes the beach.

ISHQ'ALLAH

Today we sit by the water
and listen to *Ishq'allah* on the twin headsets,
sealed off from the passing world in its silent drama —
the joggers, the fathers playing Saturday morning catch
with their sons, the spiky shadows of cormorants
on the sculpture. I had never heard it at this pitch
or volume before, an ocean of sound crashing
into our ears, a cry for change
soaring up out of the cymbals and the chant
like a soprano's cry, lifting us out of our lives.

My friend, tell me I haven't wasted
ten years of this life,
that I haven't been asleep all this time —
tell me a decade is nothing more
than an exhaled breath, the slow blink of a giant's eye.

The music batters me with its beauty
and I close my eyes against the sun,
the silver thaw of codeine seeping through my veins —
joggers suspended in the slow-moving light,
lilac-coloured sky, a river of pollen
blowing in currents along the seawall.

Above, clouds pass like continents,
their shadows flattened over the earth —
ships in full sail, giant black-winged birds
like postcards from the subconscious,
staining the sunny shore.

Tell me there's another place for us,
another chance, a parallel universe where people live
as if each day will never come again.

Is it too late to wake,
is it too late in the week to start again?
The same flood of notes storms your head, rising
like holy music in a high cathedral.

BLUE HERON

Tonight the blue heron came
to sit beside me at the water's edge.

False Creek was flat as a lake, a silver slant
of reflective foil, negative images of towers

and sailboats in the mirroring water.
The heron stood on a slick rock

and began to groom himself, casting a coy
glance in my direction. Lamps in offices

and apartments glowed in the gathering gloom
like cut-outs in paper lanterns.

We stayed like that for a long while,
like a husband and wife in front of television —

the heron on his rock, his shadow
pooling at his feet, me on my stone step.

We kept a companionable silence,
two creatures occupying the same stretch

of seawall, the same breath of existence.
His coat of feathers was stormy blue

like rocks in shallow water, rubbed silk,
ancient coins. The hour we shared

already sliding into the past —
where the sky is torn, the clouds

stained with rain.

WHAT WAS LOST
(or, Bungling the Interview for the Position of Poet
Laureate)

In cases of depression, the letter writer
writes, one should always ask
what has been lost — for days after the interview
I asked myself this, in the concrete
and ash landscape of after. It had been
a glorious morning, the kind of day
the poets praise. The willows were budding
along False Creek — soon the trees
would shake loose their showers of pollen,
soon the hesitant sun would bathe
the seawall in plum-coloured light.
Even a critic would have found it difficult
to deny the blessing —
the sleek head of a seal pup
fishing in the marina,
the dappled water shot through
with shafts of bamboo and grain,
the maple-sweet air drenched in bright.
Then the hour in the boardroom, the stumble
and fumble for words that flew
out of my head like panicked birds
as the jury's faces flickered and dimmed.
Afterwards, I wanted to forget
what was lost, to forget the day —
to say it didn't matter, it was worthless anyway.
Stepping back into the city on the cusp
of spring, carrying loss
like a hard blue pebble in my palm.

WILLOW

We've lived a long time in one place.
Even the poets are growing old.
Tonight, a student stood at the microphone
reading "Piling Blood" as lovingly
as if it were his own, and I remembered
Al Purdy's last readings packed to the rafters,
he could hardly take a sip of breath
in those crowded rooms, every event sold out
in the possibility it would be his last.
I remembered his letters, the way the period key
on his typewriter punched through the page
so that if you held it up to the light
his words would form a firmament
scattered with stars. Goh Poh Seng,
you and I are still here,
stubborn as cactus on sere ground.
Tonight your son wheeled you into the library
where two years ago you came leaning on his arm.
Your face starved to the beauty of a monk's —
I reached to embrace you but was afraid you'd dissolve
in my arms, scatter in a swirl of gold dust.
I held your hand instead, a dry leaf in mine.
When I asked if you were well, you nodded
well enough —
as if a grain of rice was sufficient,
no need for life's greedy buffet.
Around you, the storm of Parkinson's raged on
so that you swayed violently like a willow
and I was afraid to let go, hanging on
to your hand like a lifeline, your slight body
the clapper inside a ringing bell.

I am fortunate, you said, your voice
already the rush of the wind through the trees.

A GRAIN OF RICE

My father once plucked a grain of rice
from his porcelain bowl, suspended it
between wooden chopsticks —
this pale nub like a cell, a sickly
white worm, grub. His instruction
was to chew it slowly, savour it,
let the starch release and dissolve —
he wanted to teach the child
that even a grain of rice
could yield a store of sweetness
if you were starving. I tasted syrup,
molasses, a lash of vinegar.
Perhaps the body holds a genetic memory
of hunger, lack and privation
stamped into its neurons —
peasants starving to death in the parched
countryside, stuffing their mouths
with seeds, grass, hissing insects.
In my twenties, in the plenitude
of the western world, locked
in self-imposed starvation, I would reel
down the too-bright street in a daze,
gaze at anyone with food in their hands —
molecules of salt and grease and sugar
exploding like dandelions in the breeze,
I breathed and breathed,
wanting to claw their fat-smeared faces
like a wild beast after a trek through frozen tundra.
My mother's family in China shared a single
scrawny chicken on feast day,
hacked into bony pieces,

feeding two adults and twelve children.
Once I devoured a whole chicken in the bathtub —
slimy skin, rich barbecued flesh,
bitter hidden innards —
tearing it apart with my hands,
tossing the bones overboard.
Vomiting a village's dinner into the toilet.

FROZEN

The last time I saw my father
he smiled at me, and when I stood there stone-faced
behind black glasses and a veil
of Valium, he frowned and turned away,
stiff as a general in his funeral suit,
the severe lines of his body a correction
and a reprimand. Earlier, they had walked past us
on the gravel path, my mother and father,
not stopping, not stumbling in recognition.
I could see the part in my mother's hair,
the tender stripe of scalp laid bare.
Fifteen years was a long time —
long enough to become a stranger, a ghost,
to go from someone real
to something dreamed.
We gathered beside the plain wooden box.
Damp cold crept up from the earth,
the manicured green, gripping my feet like ice.
A handful of dirt blew from my fist
onto the pine coffin where my aunt lay,
tucked into herself like a foetus
or a sleeping child. Clouds scrolled
across the lowering sky.
We paid our respects, hurried back to the car.
I watched my father through the windshield —
he was handsome, this man,
almost close enough to touch.
I watched him through the fogged glass
and the shining air. The first time in fifteen years,
the last time in this life. We hadn't said a word
to each other. I looked and looked at him.

READING FIONA LAM'S *Enter The Chrysanthemum*

It was years before you looked at me
and said her name. *Do you remember my mother?*
She was a family physician, Dr. Wei . . .
Of course! Your face was her face, minus
the crumple of exhaustion, the stethoscope
and the crisp white coat.
It might have been your hands
that measured and lifted my small body
onto the scale, that pressed a cold
silver coin to my heart, that tilted my tonsils
to the examining light.

Once, she teased as she ushered me
into the reception room,
What do you want to be when you grow up?
Maybe a doctor like me, hmm?
and I burst out,
I'm going to be a writer.
The flash of electricity in my father's
mud eyes. How he bowed and scraped
as we fled the scene of my dishonour —
the esteemed doctor had proffered
her profession to me, and I had rejected it
as if saving lives was a lesser thing
than pinning words to a page.
Outside, on Broadway, the summer day detonated.

Yet all along, you were living a parallel life.
There you were, curled in the closet,
furled tight as a bud in the bedroom,

hunched over a box of bitter chocolates
while the storms swept through your house.
After you swallowed it all
and headed to law school, and I flailed
in newfound freedom on the streets,
our mothers sat for hours in the medical office —
confessing, blaming, who knows what they shared.
*It's like my daughter sprang
from a stone,* my mother would say.

Dr. Wei came to see me, just once,
at a reading years ago —
a small woman hunched in dun clothes,
retired, part blind, perhaps the beginnings
of dementia already blooming through her brain.
The organizers didn't know what to do
when she cornered me like a fortune teller
with bad news. *So sad,* she sighed,
I feel so sorry for you. So sad.
I laughed her off the way one does
the harmless hermit, the cat lady —
though years of poetry-writing poverty later,
her words would seem those of an oracle,
uncovering a grim future in the clouded crystal.

Now I am reading your book with a fist
clamped over my mouth to hold back the cries.
Your mother raging through the house,
raining recriminations on the bowed head
of your father. Your mother ministering
in the middle of the night to other mothers'
children, their measles and fevers,
while her own huddled untended and unfed.
Your mother on the phone, howling
inside the hurricane of the dementia —

Help me, help me.
My doctor. Her dry, lined hands
soft as chamois on my child's body,
as if I were a princess,
precious cargo, her own.

GRANDMOTHER

Today the news came: Grandmother was dead.
I rummaged through my body for a nub
of hurt, the way you might scour your teeth
with the tip of your tongue, searching
for the sore spot, the microscopic hole
in the dentine, the fracture along the gumline.
Found nothing. She hadn't spoken in years,
frozen and mute after a series of strokes —
this commander of twelve captives
whose favourite thing, my aunt admitted
with a sigh, was to yell.
She was famous for it, her voice a boombox
blasting songs of excoriation —
it echoed up and down the block
of that scorched California town,
boomeranging around the stucco houses
and cement gardens, a Chinese opera
of injustice and lamentation.
It would begin the moment she woke,
a growl behind the shut door
rumbling to a roar that ground on
until she brushed her teeth at night,
recriminations spat out
between mouthfuls of mint. My aunts,
her daughters, dominant in their own households,
wove around her like wraiths,
lips crimped, eyes downcast,
whispering in the wake of her wrath.
Wary of making a sound or gesture
that would set off the fusillade of blame.

Yet she never yelled at me, her first grandchild.
Praised the biscuits I baked in her kitchen
that summer I was ten, fluffy butter
and flaky pastry collapsing in her mouth.
It seemed I was on the proper path —
so clever I knew the phrases on Wheel of Fortune
before Vanna White could reveal another letter;
so reassuringly plain a cousin had to ask
if I was girl or boy.
Grandmother still remembered the time,
as a toddler, I took care of her —
clutching her hand on the way to the store,
her bosom and stomach a warm bulwark,
her gold-toothed face beaming down at mine,
I had yelped and yanked her to a stop
just before she stepped into a mud puddle.
All day she praised me, as though I'd plucked her
from the precipice. Decades later,
wheelchair-bound, she flung out her good arm
to halt a great-grandchild from tumbling
off the kitchen table to the tile floor.

Part Two:
Dear Updike

ON LOOKING INTO JOHN UPDIKE'S
Endpoint

Reading your last poems, the air
in the solarium closes in. Early spring,
trees sagging with pollen.
Crocuses and snowdrops, purple and white
bundles of blooms neat as nosegays
rooted in the earth. Papery daffodils
lit on their long tapers.
The magnolia's fleshy furred buds
like chrysalises fermenting,
the life inside them pulsating, tumbling.
What would you make of this city
you never visited, where I've dutifully lived my life
as if there were no others?

A haze of pink barely detectable
in the stand of cherry trees,
spun sugar, chemical mist.
Cotton and lint in the breeze,
a thick tickling in the throat;
plant after plant exploding open
with cargoes of allergens lethal
as peanut dust, gusts of yellow pollen.
And the rashes! Blooming across my body
like Rorschachs, a world map of hived continents.

At night I writhe in bed in an orgy of itching,
sink at last into dry-mouthed Benadryl sleep,
the floral air semi-solid, too dense with particles
to suck through the lungs. Even a cracked window
shifts the balance between inside

and outside atmospheres, spores
and dander leak in, a poisoned blessing.

You died of lung cancer in winter, writing poems
from your hospital bed in Boston.
This spring, in a world bereft
of your gaze, I grope through a fog
of antihistamines, choke on too much life.

UPDIKE REDUX

Rain is grace; rain is the sky condescending to the earth.
   — John Updike, "A Soft Spring Night in Shillington"

The sound of rain made you *happy almost to tears.*
Here, it's November again. Lightning in the night,
the neighbour's coughing through the drywall,
the tinny sounds of late night TV.
I try to remember gratitude, the wonder you felt
as a boy crouched under a wicker chair
on a porch in Shillington, storm showers falling
all around you like a benediction.
Is it possible we never met?
Perhaps your sleeve brushed mine, once,
in the desert where you spent the winter —
among the crowds on the baked streets
of Scottsdale, the avid tourists
and fake cowboys, you a tall man with a hawk nose,
skin red from psoriasis and sun.
Or perhaps we drove past your house
in the foothills of Tucson on our way back
from the Biosphere, microwave lines of heat
radiating above the road
as we crossed the dry riverbeds
toward the saguaro forest at sunset —
the talcum kiss of the parched air,
lurid watercolours in the sky. No,
this was April, you were in Beverly Farm,
it was the last spring of your life.
Here the soil sizzles, soaking up the downpour
after the Indian summer that lingered
like it would never end. Blue days of bluster

43

and blown leaves. The tree in the courtyard
a massed bruise, magenta and mauve,
the maples filtering blood through their spun keys.
If it was hard to be happy then, tell me how
to survive the winter. Tell me how
to get to Plow Cemetery, where soft fistfuls
of your ashes were scattered on stone.
Clouds of ashes, the colour of smoke and dust,
lifting above the land
you loved so much, seeding with rain.

DEAR UPDIKE

I dreaded those future aeons when I would not be present —
an endless succession of days I would miss, with their own
news and songs and styles of machine.
   — John Updike, "On Being a Self Forever"

No, nothing much has changed.
A year later, the world is still one you'd recognize —
no winged cars to clog the air,
no robots to do our dirty work.
The hours and days, as it turns out,
just go on. No space age fabrics
drape our tired bodies, though I did try on a sweater
built of bamboo, soft as chewed silk.
The chrome surface of the dream's lake
where I swim every night
still hides the same wreckage in its mud bottom.
Sometimes I open my eyes at the morning
and wonder what words you would wring
from the splendour and boredom
of these limited hours. Some day
there'll be a future we won't recognize,
but not now. Outside my window,
the low moan of winter in the ragged street.
Flakes of funereal ash falling from the sky.
The soiled comforters of the clouds;
the tightly wrapped buds of winter roses.
These grudging gifts of December,
tied in newsprint. For weeks after your death,
The *New Yorker* continued to print your backlog
as if death couldn't stopper your creativity,
as if you were still writing in that midnight room.
But not a word from you now, and it's dark at four.

UPDIKE IN PENNSYLVANIA

Best wishes for you and your work, you wrote once
in your careful, cramped hand.
There's been no work for weeks.
I sleep away the afternoons like a cancer patient
blasted by radiation, wake sour-mouthed
and tachycardic, swallowing bile
and a bulge of panic in the throat.

This day won't go away —
the same fuzzed carpet, blank wall,
the shiv of sun in the mirror
slicing like a migraine.
In Shillington, the dogwood tree at the side
of your childhood home is in bloom, a plume
of salmon smoke puffing higher
than the rooftop, singeing the shingle eaves.

Soon the English professors will descend on Pennsylvania,
seeking out the sources of your inspiration —
the poorhouse wall, a slab of crumbled stone;
the scratched side of a barn, pieced together like a puzzle;
the pagoda serrating the sky above Reading.

I was there, once, miles from Shillington —
drenched green fields, the jewel boxes of red barns
beaming in the sun, clouds paddling across the sky.
The wary faces of Amish men
perched like royalty in the back seats of their neighbours' cars,
crabby as crows in strange black garments —

They test your patience sometimes, my driver sighed,
always showing up at the back door to store
food in your fridge, borrow your telephone,
beg a ride into town. I was drunk
on the apple-cider air, sailing along
the back roads through Updike country —

HOSPICE OF THE NORTH SHORE, DANVERS, MA

Mr. Updike, a long-time resident of Beverly Farm, died of lung cancer at Hospice of the North Shore in Danvers, said his wife, Martha.
     — *The Boston Globe*, January 27, 2009

Pictures float up on the pond
of the computer screen like water flowers.
Jangly music, meant to soothe,
accompanies the virtual tour.
This is the closest I will come
to your last days, peering like a pervert
into your final privacy
on the opposite shore. Here is the hospice,
in New England shades of storm and surf —
maiden sculpture in verdigris,
lollipop disc of stained glass,
burble of water on stone. By night
it appears a glamorous mansion, windows ablaze
as if Gatsby and his guests were alive again
in an endless jazz age
of champagne toasts, tennis whites.
After the foursquare house in Shillington
your residences dotted the eastern seaboard
until you arrived here, in these rooms
at the end of the world —
the cheerfully named "Country Kitchen"
where plump staff serve up meatloaf and apple pie;
the guest lobby whose tabletop Easter lily,
milky blooms trumpeting the air,
hints at a life

after life. Walls mustard in one light,
sunshine in another. Rooms with patio doors
flung wide, light coursing inside;
the Amish quilts on the single beds
a homey touch from Pennsylvania.
A kaleidoscope of faces, familiar and anodyne,
rotating above you. Medicines
and ministrations, the seductive tug
of sedation, morphine tastier than any penny candy.
The furniture in the room miraculous
for being the last furniture you would ever see.
It's said that hearing is the last sense
to go, that the dead hear the rustle
of the sheet drawn over their face, the priest's
footsteps across the floor, a window tugged shut.
Of course you still had more to say —
you who lovingly delineated
every moment of your life, who believed
that *words could save a life*. Was there a pen,
a pad of paper bedside, or were you finally
past all that? The ocean of words
you swam in every morning of your life —
was it there for you, blue and buoyant
to the end, or did you find yourself stranded
on a soda-white shoal, in the silence
of outer space?

THINKING OF U(PDIKE)

In Summerland, the hours of silence are long.
Even this one life, said to be over in a day,

holds space that stretches to the horizon.
Abundance, then a harvest of loss —

berries in a bowl, plucked from an orchard
sagging with fruit, then the fires

sweeping across the sky above Kelowna.
Each summer perhaps the last, yet I can't

love the world any more than this.
The view from a bridge, a thousand windows

shining in the salty sun.
The wind in the trees, a tangle of sweet water;

silver sage and burnt lavender
to scent our sleep. The bitter cream of almonds.

Someday I will stand on the lawn
of the hospice where you died,

the cemetery where your ashes were scattered.
Someday I will make that pilgrimage,

like a stranger who loved you. Let my eyes
hold the last thing your eyes held

in their vision, mottled wall or crumbed carpet,
the beauty of it all rushing in, too late.

Part Three:
Lost and Found

SWIMMING LESSONS

The white doves flew in
and out of the trees below our balcony.
In our room we were fighting.
It was nothing, you said, *just a silly crack,*
it meant less than nothing —
a crack through which one moment slid
into another, swift as the sunset
in Honolulu. One moment the green Pacific
at our feet and then night,
sea and sky a thick blanket
thrown over the homes around Diamond Head.
The next afternoon the wave that knocked us both over
at Waikiki Beach stole my Fendi sunglasses —
and for a moment I wished
it had been a person instead, drowned
and swept away by the undercurrent, even someone
I knew but liked only a little, not like
I loved those glasses. The wave closed over
and over my head, I swallowed salt water
like medicine for a sore throat,
the sky suddenly miles above
and my body locked inside this watery room,
thrashing in a blue and airless bed.
So this was what it was like,
no time for remorse or reflection,
only an animal dying,
all helpless instinct and fear.
I struggled back to shore
where you stood, hand held over
your eyes, looking in every direction
but this one.

HONOLULU

This is the memory you will take home —
the man sprawled on the ground
in front of the International Market,
paramedics kneeling next to him
like ministering angels. Not even Lady Gaga
blaring beneath the banyan tree
can drown out his bellows. All you see of him
are his legs, rigid, corded with veins,
deeply tanned like a retiree's
who spends his days at golf.
For once the vendors are silent
as they stand vigil next to their stalls
clamorous with trinkets —
walls of glow-in-the-dark magnets,
garlands of artificial leis,
battery-operated birds flapping
through the humid air.
A puppy made in China
nuzzles your foot, bead eyes blinking,
nylon tail wagging.
How quiet the vendors are, the only time
they will be still this whole day —
struck dumb by the sobriety
of the moment, as if this stranger
had invited them to a funeral, his own.
His shouts of pain or protest
seeming to come from some unearthly place,
some future hell that would find them
even here in this touted paradise.

When he was carted away
the commerce began again, like the bright chatter
of birds that had been disrupted
by a stone thrown in their midst.
A vendor shows you a T-shirt
embedded with an LED panel, blinking
a scarlet heart even in the dark.
Tank tops with clever, cruel slogans:
I speak Engrish. He's gay.
Thank God I'm pretty.
At the entrance to the market
where the man was propped like a mascot,
a welcoming god, a pool of his urine
stains the dusty brick. Later it will be covered
by a stand of flyers advertising
luaus, scuba dives, Polynesian dinner shows.

MAUI

Remember the plump dove in the banyan tree,
nestled like a blown flower between the root columns,
not his starved cousins pecking our toes in the market;
the thickets of golden bamboo
on our hot hike to Twin Falls,
not the disappointing destination, twin dribbles
of water into a dank grotto.

Today, fires in the hills of West Maui.
Smoke choked above the serenity pool,
spark and smoulder
in the shrubby ridges. Seaside cliffs
perfumed with plumeria,
hedges pinned with starry blooms
like planets in the night sky.
Waves bubbling over black lava rocks,
crumble of charcoal.

A bird comes to share your breakfast
on the lanai — tufted red cardinal
stalks the table with a studied look
of disinterest, circles your plate while pretending
to peer in other directions, then chirps
in gratitude for the muffin crumbs.
At nightfall, frogs kick their legs
in the lotus pond, lavender and lime flowers
wink fireworks in the murky water.

The locals crowd the beachside shacks
at sunset, tracking in a day's worth of grime
from the shore, hair ropy with seawater,

skin barnacled with salt crystals,
dipped in a sugar crust of sand —
shipwrecked sailors strung with shells,
tattooed with symbols, bedraggled with blooms.
Who you might be if you started again.

SEDONA BLUES

I.

The flat motel air.
Lying across the bed, listening to a family
play Marco Polo in the kidney pool.
The desert a dry rasp in the throat,
soft burrs buried in skin.
A scrape of red rock
against the cratered earth. I wake in the night
forgetting how to breathe again,
stumble past your sleeping form
into the yellow cave of the bathroom.
Where have the people
who populated my young life gone?
Boxes in the ground, handfuls
of ash in the wind. Give me an incantation
to shake their spirits, a magic word
or crystal spell. The glittering rocks
in the New Age stores lie coal-black
and silent in my palm.

II.

The desert doesn't want us.
Bakes my skin to cracked terracotta,
spears a cactus prickle so deep between your toes
it takes an hour to extract, sweat stinging my eyes.
Blood leaks into our mouths
from our parched nostrils.
Here the dead are all around us:
bear faces in a basket at the trading post,

bins of raccoon bones, pheasant claws,
badger skulls. The clay earth
stains our sandals with rust.
Driving to Tucson past clumps of cacti,
"The Star-Spangled Banner"
on the radio at noon, the hot breath
of the desert hunts us down.

III.

How could anything flower here,
but it does — the stone and spike
of cacti force out sleepy roses,
cottonwood clouds haze the air.
The ocotillo's tongues of flame
on the tips of thorny spears
lick at the tile sky.
These are the gifts the desert gives us:
blazing days and freezing nights,
heat rash and prickly pear blooms
like brimming bowls of grace.
A field of saguaro at sunset,
ranks of green soldiers on the mountainside,
arms raised over the skeleton ribs of the fallen.

LAS VEGAS

Ghost of smoke in the hallways.
Sour stench in the woodwork, behind the gleam
of renovation, the bamboo wallpaper,
gilt mirrors, the bed sealed in its envelope
of laundered linens. A dubious history.

Fremont Street, second tier to the Strip —
toothy showgirls in bedraggled tail-feathers,
pint-sized cartoon characters mugging for photos
and spare change. In the souvenir store a bear,
costume head tucked under his arm,
pays for a Red Bull and a fifth
of vodka. Sludge of spilled drinks underfoot,
a sticky river of sugar and slurry ice
glazing the first paved street in Vegas.

On stage a magician thrusts his arm,
his leg, his whole upper body
through a box of whirring steel blades
and half the audience wanders away,
suspecting a con. Nowhere for a tired tourist
to sit but at a slot machine, numb
to the jingle-jangle, the grind and swivel.

The girls of the Glitter Gulch boast banners
across their bare chests that shout "Humph!"
and "Indeed!", as if this was some other world,
fifty years ago. Above, an American rocket
burns across the electric sky,
this canopy of twelve million lights,
shooting for the moon.

CHRISTMAS DAY, CANNON BEACH

All night the winds howled through the town,
the windows shook in their frames,
I dreamt of towering waves and our slow drift
off the surface of the earth,
among fragments of houses
returning to timber. You lay next to me
like a sleeping dog, a beast with hot skin
and matted hair, churning in your own turmoil.
When I rested my hand on your stomach
the engine of your life hummed.
Ahead, the new year with its schedule
of disasters and emergencies.
Who are the people who live on this coast
yet are nowhere to be seen at dusk
or dawn, faces turned to the watery light?
If I had a house on the beach
you would find me here day or night
like a lamp always lit, looking out
towards the island of seagulls,
white ghosts stranded
on the other side of the frozen river.
In morning the ocean is full
of sky and storm, carrying the town
wave by wave out to sea.
The sand shifts under our feet,
drowned by marine foam,
marbled like raku, mica swirling into clay.
The sand spirals up
to sting our faces in a whirling storm,
the wind combs the blond beach grass,
the wind tears the words from your mouth.

BEST WESTERN

It wakes you in the night, this mystery
that might be a calling card
from your own death.
It follows you to California,
tolling in the hotel room's half-light
so that you sit upright,
the gas flame twitching in the fireplace,
the royal palms stark
against the charred horizon.
This body you'd ignored for so long —
all the while it was living
its own life, its murmured complaints building
to a pressure in the chest so grave
you think of the medieval torture
where men were pressed to death
under rocks, not an avalanche
of weight but a steady accretion,
the granite pile growing, so that it took
three days to die. Three days!
What dreams and fevers did the men endure?
Here at the Best Western, footsteps in the room above.
Trickling water from a flushed toilet,
a hidden pipe —
somehow you've lived half a life
without understanding how the world works,
taking for granted the gush of water
from the faucet, fresh and potable,
the surge of electricity into a switched lamp,
the tidy funnelling away of waste
down the drain. All these systems
in place as if only for your comfort —

you who once watched a documentary
on a tribe in Africa, pygmies
who shimmied up tree trunks
to lap rainwater from the tree's crotch,
whose daily work
involved this endless pursuit of water.
Now it seems a form of ingratitude, to know
so little of this material world
you couldn't fix a leaky pipe,
let alone build a house around your sorry self
to keep out the storm.
A form of shame, to stumble
through this life without knowing the names
of everything. And what of this body?
Could you even locate your liver?
The pressure clamps your chest,
blood pours through the pulsing chamber,
something hidden explodes in the red depths
like a charge detonated out of sight.
Of course it's too late
for the small vows you make,
the deals with gods or devils,
the absurd desire to start from scratch —
this scuttled life you'd transform
into one of grace, given another chance.
This life you'd live among the African pygmies,
sucking dusty stones for saliva,
licking dew off spiky leaves,
joyfully, if that was the only life you were given.

LOST AND FOUND

Somehow the custom orthotic, a slip of plastic
worth hundreds of dollars, worked its way out
of my sandal in the rough landscape
of the lunar beach and hid
amidst sandcastles and fire pits,
chips of charcoal and tangles of kelp.
We combed and combed the shore,
the waning light against us. Watermelon moon
in the cotton candy sky. It seemed then
that this life was a collection of losses,
a slipping down an ever steeper slope,
shedding possessions and loved ones until,
at the last, we shed our own mottled coat of flesh,
this ragged lumpy lived-in self.
Where had the California beauty gone,
though the sun was setting
behind the lifeguard's blue hut,
the surf drumming? All we found
was what others had lost —
a sneaker, two battered cellphones,
a guitar pick wedged into the sand
like a tiny surfboard. Row of burnt palms
behind the lighthouse, decomposing sea lion
in the rank breeze.

The next morning we returned to the beach,
holding out hope like metal detectors, and there,
in front of me, gleaming like the foot-bone
of an exotic animal, the orthotic!
To find something, after so many losses!
The photograph of that moment shows me

with arms raised in religious ecstacy,
eyes closed and mouth open in a half-mad
silent song of hallelujah. You would have thought
I was calling down the spirits from the next world.
That someone I loved had come back to me
from the place where no one returns. Here in Santa Cruz,
where a man in rags shakes his finger
at the heavenly blue sky, shouting,
Your mother was a hamster,
and your father smelled of elderberry!

GUANACASTE JOURNAL

Horses gallop the beach, flying past like figures in a dream.

*

We are sheltered from the country at the oceanfront resort.
We are miles down a gravel road where black figures loiter
under the constellatory trees in a hail of seed pods.
Costa Rica passes outside the window of the night bus —
small lit homes flaring in the scrubby landscape,
doors open in the equatorial heat, bare tiled floors.
Coffee farm, cantaloupe farm.
Our ghost reflections in the glass, the white gawp
of tourist stares. Maids squatting on the curb
at the guarded gate, then the hotel rising out of the tropical
night like a castle in Las Vegas.

*

The heat erases everything, like the deliverance
of morphine. The walk from the resort
to Matapalo Beach a cartoon crawl through the desert —
even the palms wilt in this heat, yellow as sunflowers.
Flammable skin. Clack of palm fronds,
crickets making their orchestral music.
Chapel-white hotel against a blue sky
strewn with butterflies. Grasshoppers lining
the butter-cream corridors. Surely this is no place for sorrow?

*

Across the water, tens of thousands
of Haitians perish in the earthquake rubble.
We'd know more if we watched the news,
the pleas for aid, the images of children stumbling
around collapsed buildings where their whole families
are buried, but we have our own grief.
What would we do with someone else's,
where would we carry it on our bodies?
Already the doctor says I am too heavy.

*

We are intent on leisure, teams of tan people
at our service, rousing us to water sports and aerobics,
salsa and magic tricks on the show stage.
In the pool we swim up to the bar, sit chest-deep in water
with our pina coladas, this was someone's idea
of paradise. A tangle of toilet paper swirls past
in the chlorinated water. A wasp paddles frantically
on the chemical surface, unimpressed
by this blue heaven. Rum floats on my tongue.
We take shelter by the artificial waterfall,
in the shade cast by a plastic boulder.

*

A man who looks like John Updike sits next to me
at breakfast. Updike, I am staring at the sea,
under the sun that was your psoriatic skin's salvation.
The women, their shapes and sizes, their moles
and cellulite you would have detailed in your desire
to *get it all down*, to love it all. The cantaloupe breasts
of a young girl on an old woman wearing a gold bikini.
The aging men in their unashamed half-nakedness,
wrinkly buttocks and pot bellies, white hairs sprouting
from dank crevices. Some days I see you everywhere,
you who never once graced my sight while you were alive.

*

The food! The buffet is an ocean spilling its shores -
vats and cornucopias and platters of food,
proteins and starches, sweets and tree fruits,
seafood prepared a dozen ways, station after station
heaped with rainbow choice. Seconds and thirds.
A storm in my stomach in the middle of the night;
groaning with the consequences of gluttony.
The starving North Koreans combed through the manure
of farm animals, searching for kernels of corn.
They lived on bark stripped from trees,
rotten vegetables and handfuls of grass,
until they began to die. A day of this life
would be a celestial reward beyond imagination,
beyond hope.

*

The leatherback turtle drags herself to the base
of a braided tree to lay her eggs.
We are reverent as mourners
watching her painful progress up the beach,
the hours-long digging of the hole, flippers sending up
gusts of dust. The moon has gone missing,
though the sky is gasping with stars.
Stars reflected in the water like the lanterns
of drowned boats. The next day the eggs hatch,
the baby turtles scurry one by one to the sea,
past the gauntlet of tourists snapping photos -
they make their blind heedless way to their destination,
tumbling end over end in their haste
to escape that boy's greedy grasp,
that woman's clumsy feet, our cries and clicking cell phones.
A wonder they survive us, anything
survives us. The first wave sweeps them off
to other perils.

                    *

Float in a boat down the river. Howler monkeys
in the treetops, swinging through the leafy canopy.
Monkeys with golden faces sipping the silty water
at the riverbank, crocodile's beady eyes
above the waterline like air bubbles, pagoda tail.
Iguanas in sunset colours, tangerine
and lemon, a china bird on legs like flamingo stilts.
A row of bats tattooed on a tree trunk,
forming a pattern like a snake to scare off predators.
They know what to do to survive. Later,
we drink guava juice in the cactus garden,

provide sustenance for insects with whirring wings
helicoptering through the sandstorm.

*

You start to recognize them at the buffet,
along the beach and on the tour bus -
these strangers sealed under the dome with us,
in this world away from the world.
Their paperback novels and Kindles,
their holiday clothes blazing with flowers
and palm trees. They have earned these carnival pleasures
with honest labour, some of them.
Beside me, the American on the deck chair poolside
busies her hands with a bundle of yarn. I think
a gift for a grandchild, but no,
she is knitting scarves and toques
for the homeless. *We gave everything we had*,
she says of the drive to collect winter clothes,
but the need is still there, so now she is knitting
her donations. Was I wrong about everyone?

*

Aftershocks in Haiti. The storms are moving
down the coast.

Part Four:
Fear of Falling

Spring, fall, summer, winter: a life as well as a year has its seasons.
— John Updike, "Introduction", *Rabbit Angstrom: A tetralogy*

ENGLISH BAY

Again we found ourselves at the shoreline,
among shards of shell and plastic,
scrim of seaweed trapping my feet like a net.
Red freighters and the grey Onley mist of the islands.
The seashell gleam of sun on water, herringbone sky.
I was thinking of a movie where a man was drowning
in the middle of the ocean, huge swells soaring
all around him like dunes in a desert, and how I'd once said,
That's what it feels like, grief —
years ago, before anyone had even died.
Who knew how wide the ocean would get,
how high those waves would climb.
Then I went into the water, into that marine world
of kelp and plankton. The green that bathed my legs
had travelled for miles to reach this bay.
A noose of cloud hung on the gold horizon.
Spores, sand in the gritty air. No one I loved was there.

SUMMERLAND

Water to the left of the winding highway,
sage mesa to the right, the peaks like steeples
and temples, palace ruins, architecture
of lost civilizations. Holes in the cliffs,
bone-coloured in the fading light,
gophers snoring inside their dens.
At night the lake throws black paint
onto the shore. The dock dwindles,
the sky is sanded with stars.
I want the dense dark, to dive down
where the silver ladder drops, where the stumps
of the crumbled wharf sprout branches
underwater, ghostly limbs grasping
for air. Among rusted bicycles
and bottles shapeless as sea glass.
You visit me in dreams, in the shadow hours
where I skim the surface of sleep,
in the pearl-gray half-light.

Last night you set yourself on fire —
still the pain of your physical body
couldn't extinguish the other pain.
It's just a body, you said. Seeping blisters
stuck to the sheets, skin and seared flesh
pressed a pattern like bloody handprints
or red-veined leaves onto the comforter.
Never again to hear your voice on the phone,
to know even that of your presence.
I'd ask for less. You on the other side of the world,
incommunicado, alive in a cold cell
cut into a barren hillside. But alive.

These Okanagan nights spent skating in circles,
drifting aimlessly in a leaky boat —
waiting for sleep that ducks and dodges,
waiting to plunge down into the depths.
But then we unlock the front door,
and at the end of the harlequin hallway
is the square of blue, the lake —

THE MUSIC OF WRECKAGE

Passing by the park this morning,
I saw heaps of matchstick timber,
gouged walls, the alley inlaid with smashed glass —
they were tearing down the sculptors' studio.
I hadn't thought of you in days. Weeks.
So this is how life goes on, heartlessly,
abandoning its dead like clothes gone out of fashion.

Now the gaping jaws of the bulldozers
gobbled great mouthfuls out of the building
where you once worked in bronze,
your wax castings malleable as mercury,
each female form a buttery handful
cupped in your palm.
The back wall was still standing,
like a remnant from a stage set;
piles of dusty pink bricks like coral reef
littered a glittering fake beach.
A reek of decayed wood wrinkled the air.
The construction workers, mere boys
with shifty adolescent faces, couldn't conceal
their joy in all that destruction —
the nervy thrill of heavy machinery, splinters of glass
reflecting the sky, the lot a giant sandbox
sparked with peril. I watched the sign on the studio,
askew, tilt and tumble down. Went on my way.

But from my condo a block away I could still hear
the music of wreckage, a low rumble
through double-paned windows —
the chewing, the gnashing of glass

and crunching of metal. The space that once held you ground down to sand in days.

LIFE AFTER DEATH

The world closes over its dead,
folds them into compost —
or else they scatter to nothing, particles as fine as silt
on its winds and waters. The cheerful Maritime pub
where we said good-bye for the last time
is now a sports bar blasting out
the ultimate fighting championships.
The studio where you sculpted
now a chopped iron sea of rubble. Two years later,
your partner and I have become friends —
as if grief were a sisterhood, a familial tie,
as if some of the same sluggish blood
of life after death
circulated in our veins.
In this way, you remain.
Traces of you still glimmer, here and there
in this living world.
Your watch hangs heavy on her wrist,
thick metal and blue dials,
ticking the indifferent time.
Tonight she gives me a zucchini
from her garden, a warty green monster that thrills
with its ugly flesh, bulging out of the soil
behind the last house you bought.
What wonders this half-life still holds.
Her hand, icy from her frozen drink,
coming to rest on the back of my neck
like a salve, a cold compress
for a fever that won't break.

THE BEGINNING OF SPRING

The day you collapsed at your desk,
I was running errands a block away —
ducking into the deli at The Bay
for a coconut bun and an apple tart,
sampling the season's offerings at H&M and Winners,
standing in line at London Drugs
with an allergy prescription.

Spring was rampant,
seeping into stone corners
                              and charcoal alleyways,
drowsing in plots of sun-drunk tulips.
A canopy of cherry blossoms overhead,
gorged balls of puff and tinsel;
the wax lanterns of the magnolia tree;
explosions of rhododendrons.

At your desk, in the firm where you'd worked
for thirty years, it was a day like any other
in that glass box in the sky.
                              Now fire trucks
and ambulances shriek past, bells clanging.
The air shakes, scatters into pastel confetti.
The horizon heaves, the ocean-blue sky ripples.
The sound of your life ending scrapes my ears in passing —

The day you collapsed at your desk.

MEMORIAL

We stand in ranks like soldiers,
the great hall bodied with light even on this drear day.
A wake-up call, one lawyer whispers
to another about your collapse at work,
and perhaps this is what they are all thinking —
that it could have happened to any of them.
But it happened to you. Your portrait
propped between two monumental bouquets,
your face preserved on film yet the mind behind it,
the physical body, gone.
The stone floor beneath our feet,
the winter air. Rain that slides like ice floes
down the sheets of glass.

The frost and marble, the blur of shivering light.
The army of mourners in midnight suits,
as though posing for a black and white photograph.
As though you could feel our breath and pulse where you lay,
having died in the month of your birth.
As though our multitudes could warm the vault.
Instead, the soaring space chills our hands,
numbs our lips and noses white.
The nudge of nausea in the throat.
Weariness spreading like the ice burn of opiates.
Your heart exploding like a shot apple.

VERTIGO

Sometimes it visits in the morning
and ends up staying for days.
Invisible as a headache, or depression,
more a vortex than an illness —
you turn your head, and it's there.
A tumbling in the inner ear,
then a somersault
through space, layer after layer
of air. It's like constantly stumbling
off a balcony or a bridge, it's like the dream
of plummeting through the black galaxy,
falling all night until you died
or woke. Strange things happen in the ear,
that musky unplumbed space —
silence, then a marine roar,
clicks and clatters, a weird cotton numbness
like the blank moment of stalled time
just before pain rushes in
like seawater.
Flu, a plane ride, and somehow
the bug crawled in your ear and set everything
tilt-a-whirl, the smallest movements suddenly
with planetary consequences —
standing up dangerous,
lying down worse. You have to catch hold
of the nearest solid thing and hang on
as you spin through all the space
that is the empty day ahead.

BLUE LAGOON

In painkiller dreams our hotel room faces
a blue lagoon. Celestial blue,
clear down to the white sand bottom
stuck with shards of shells striped and spotted
like chocolate eggs. I dive down like a pelican
spotting a seafood snack, pluck souvenirs
from the tropical waters, surface in a flash
of sea-spray and rainbow mist.
The sandbanks are studded with geodes,
rocks with their dull faces sheared off
to reveal cathedrals of colour, Creamsicle orange
and Kool-Aid purple, staggering masses
of crystal glitter, it takes all my strength
to prise each rock from the ledge and lunge
for the surface. Here on earth
I am bed-bound, wake thrashing in the night
from a muscle that twists and spasms.
In the bathroom I squat over the toilet
like an emu, skin sparkling with sweat,
pee dribbling down my leg.
It takes all morning to crawl into underwear
and socks, to contort into a puddle of pants.
The painkillers are from paradise,
the promised manna from heaven
that sifts over the desert like snow.

FEAR OF FALLING

At the lake resort, frogs clamour in the wetland marsh
where the beaver sleeps in a heap
of fur in his den, the muskrat cruises
across the scummed surface of the pond,

shrieking birds flash their scarlet shoulders
from tree to tree. This world goes on.
Guests stagger home from the wedding —
clatter of heels on the boardwalk, drunken laughter;

quail freeze in mid-crossing, uncertain
whether to turn back, rush into the blank beyond.
That morning we drove up Giant's Head Mountain
for the first and last time, the road

a single lane almost vertical
and the view tumbling away into vertigo,
wineries and terraced vineyards
and the blue eye of the lake set in stone.

So steep it seemed we were climbing up
to meet our own souls in heaven,
the car hugging rock and shrub while eternity
sailed past inches away, an ocean

of blue air that would fail to hold us aloft
for so much as a cartoon second
before the tourist vista below rose up
to smack us like a map swatting a bug.

My sweating palms gripped the seat,
I was thinking of Updike's lifelong fear of falling
from a plane or building, and how much more prosaic
his end turned out, drowning in his own lungs

in a hospice bed, and how the other day my body
did something it had never done before —
washing my face in the morning,
a wave of nausea crept upon the still horizon

and crashed over me, my stomach heaved
and a clot of blood burst from my mouth
into the sand-white sink.
How it can come out of the blue like that —

a lump in the breast, blood in the bowl,
heart winding down like a stopped watch.
The bulge of a tumour in the fuddled brain,
a black mole mutating, a persistent itch

with no insect or dermatitis at its source.
But the car had clung stubbornly
to the un-slippery slope.
The blood had tasted sweet, like cherry wine.

WAITING

Follow the blue arrows to Radiology —
as if this were a child's game
or a fairy tale, turn and turn again
in this bleak maze, past hollowed faces
in makeshift beds, the walking half-dead
with limbs swaddled and stiffened in casts,
fuzzed scalps topped by toques.
How shabby we all look
under the leaky fluorescent lights —
distorted as if in funhouse mirrors,
brittle-thin or bloated
as tankers, each of us carrying
some fatal flaw.

We wait in the lavender room
to be called, doubly robed, veiled from neck
to kneecap in filmy blue.
The gowns show wear —
one missing its ties, another
peppered with holes like buckshot.
Surely if there was a place for luxury,
it should be here. *Give us something
to miss about this material life, give us
sunlight through slatted blinds;
arias sung by coloraturas in sumptuous dresses;
give us one more day in the shade
of palm trees, the conversations
of painted birds overhead;
give us the banquet table groaning
with the wedding feast;
scent the island air with honeysuckle and pikake . . .*

Not the dried-out bouquet on the receptionist's desk.
Not the belches and hairy shins of my neighbours,
this collection of hobbled humanity
we've become in the scent-free zone
of the waiting room, watching "Jeopardy"
on an ancient TV, the contestants on screen
bathed in a sickly greenish hue
as if they all had the flu.

In a moment I will be called
into a bare examination room, the only ornament
nailed above the doorway —
Jesus on the cross, arched in agony.
Names float through the air
like bright scraps of paper,
slips drawn from a lottery drum.

But morning will come, again —
strands of blood swirling like helixes
in the bowl, tangled scarlet yarn,
calligraphy in crimson ink.

TO A FRIEND NEAR THE END

There's no raging *against the dying of the light.*
No rummaging through the home movie reels
of regrets and recriminations, lost loves,
a dictionary of words spoken too soon or late —
My mind just went blank, you say.
You lay in the hospital bed like a fish
on a cutting board, a corpse
in the morgue. As though you'd lived
a perfect life with no loose ends,
nothing undone —
though in the shopping centre last month
you swore the old lady hobbling by,
the one with the brightest blue eyes,
was the woman you had the affair with
decades ago. Those 1960's summer afternoons
baking at the beach while your young children
splashed the shore. But she was older than you —
She would be in a nursing home now, you say.
Or dead. Probably dead.

Forty years between us, we've been unlikely friends.
You used to tickle me with stories
of the time before ballpoint pens,
before contact lenses, before malls.
When the air was black with coal
from the factories, sprinkling your lungs
with the seeds of your death.
Now you are a collection of complaints,
your body a bewildering betrayal of joints and nerves,
aches and pains. You bend for the soap in the shower,
and throw out your back. You lie awake at night

listening to the scrabble of your stomach,
worrying about the stents in your chest,
fearing the stopped breath of sleep apnea
that will jolt your heart to its final paroxysm.
Yesterday it was the arthritis in your hip,
today the sciatica,
tomorrow a bout of bronchitis.
Already there is a whiff of the grave
in your breath, a brief stench like a calling card
from the next world.

Nature goes on unnoticed outside your window —
the herons nesting in the trees at Stanley Park,
the whitecaps on a windy day at English Bay,
the evening skies painted with pomegranate.
Slipping in and out of sleep
in front of the TV, it seems harder to rise
than to sink, to give in to the place
the soul wants to go
after 80 years on this planet.
Now you disdain the simple pleasures
that once sustained you —
the soft snap of digestive biscuits,
the sweet heat of sugared tea.
You are even losing your taste for the forbidden —
glistening strips of salty bacon,
slabs of liver soaked in sauce,
pocketfuls of tooth-pulling toffee.
My friend, what then could make you stay?

Midlife

Distance improves vision.
  — John Updike, "Midpoint"

Some days you are bored with beauty.
The sun takes decades to set.

*

Above the yellow Adirondack chairs
a cloud of gnats whirl, black dots
twisting in a spiral against the sky.
Their happy, hopping dance
a tease, a torment.

*

You waited all winter
for summer, suspended like a sickly fish
in seaweed-green water, yearning for a glint
of light at the surface.

*

Last week in the dim sum restaurant
your face in the smeared mirror
among all the black-haired heads
could have been anyone's.
Your family tragedies, any family's.

Just today you learned
your neighbour's in Afghanistan, his brother
court-martialled for shooting a wounded
Taliban fighter to end his suffering.
What made your grief so singular?

*

The couples on the seawall march on,
promenading beside the creek in a trot,
ignoring the heron on his log.
The gold unfolding on the horizon.

*

There's the sense we've been around too long,
spoiled things. These concrete towers
with shoddy windows shifting inside their frames.
The sky would not miss us if we were gone.

*

Honey in the air, shavings of cut grass,
excrement. Sweet breeze
through the lime-green trees.

*

This crowding sensation in the head,
the way words used to swarm you
like bees. Furious to escape into the world.

*

Now the long tracts of silence.
But who knows, a silence
perhaps as worthy as noisy labour,
the way the contemplation of a simple object —
bruised pear in the bowl,
lump of sea glass on the sill —
might squeeze more meaning out of the moment
than all this frantic busyness we're praised for.

*

You've come to the place of not knowing.
Surrender, maybe. Where even the enamel sky
of summer is crazed with lightning.

*

So this is your home, at midpoint —-
ruts in the faded carpet,
limp cacti dreaming of the desert,
furniture too worn to support your weight.

*

Sunspots on crumpled book-jackets,
blotches of mildew on blinds,
angry crossing-out strokes of erasure
against the grain of the cherrywood desk.

*

Decades passed.
Parking lots turned into highrises,
highrises into leaky condos.
The trees grew so tall even your neighbours disappeared.

Acknowledgments

Some of the poems in this collection previously appeared in the following publications: *The Antigonish Review, Contemporary Verse 2, Event, Geist, The Georgia Straight, The Malahat Review, Prairie Fire, Queen's Quarterly, Ricepaper, Room, subTerrain,* and *The Walrus.*

"Updike Redux" will appear in *John Updike Remembered* (University of Alabama Press).

"Fortune" was commissioned by Canada CODE. "Noise" was commissioned by re:THINK Housing Vancouver.

"The Night Market" was chosen for *Best Canadian Poetry 2009,* ed. AF Moritz. "Swimming Lessons" was chosen for *Best Canadian Poetry 2010,* ed. Lorna Crozier. "Grandmother" was chosen for *Best Canadian Poetry 2011,* ed. Priscila Uppal.

Many thanks to the BC Arts Council, for time to write. The John Updike Society, for information and photographs. My editor Ron Smith, for his thoughtful and inspired suggestions — you are every poet's dream! Randal Macnair at Oolichan Books, for his enthusiasm and commitment. John Patterson, for the den in Summerland, and for all our journeys together.

Photo: John Patterson

Evelyn Lau was born in Vancouver in 1971. She is the author of five previous volumes of poetry, two short story collections, two works of non-fiction, and a novel. *Runaway: Diary of a Street Kid*, published when she was 18, was made into a CBC movie. Lau's prose books have been translated into a dozen languages worldwide. Her poetry has been selected for inclusion in the *Best American Poetry* and *Best Canadian Poetry* anthologies, as well as receiving a National Magazine Award. *You Are Not Who You Claim* won the Milton Acorn People's Poet Award, *Oedipal Dreams* was nominated for the Governor-General's Award, and *Living Under Plastic* won the Pat Lowther Award for best book of poetry by a woman in Canada. Evelyn is the 2011-2014 Poet Laureate for the City of Vancouver.